First published 2000 AD
This edition © Wooden Books Ltd 2005 AD

Published by Wooden Books Ltd.
8A Market Place, Glastonbury, Somerset

British Library Cataloguing in Publication Data
Sullivan, D.P.
Leys

A CIP catalogue record for this book is
available from the British Library

ISBN 1 904263 38 0

Printed and bound in Great Britain by
The Cromwell Press, Trowbridge, Wiltshire.
Recycled papers supplied by Paperback.

LEYS

SECRET SPIRIT PATHS
IN ANCIENT BRITAIN

written and illustrated by

Danny Sullivan

Thanks to Ulrich Magin (p.24), Paul Bennet (p.33), Adam Dutton (p.41) and John Palmer (p.53) for permission to use their illustrations. Indirect thanks to Alfred Watkins, William Dudley, Hayward Sumner, Tom Solberg, David Mowajartai, Brian Larkman, William Stukeley and Una Woodruff.

The examples of leys in this book come from my larger volume "Ley Lines - a comprehensive guide to alignments", published by Piatkus, where the phenomenon of ancient landscape lines is explored in more depth.

Other useful sources of information are "The Old Straight Track" by Alfred Watkins, "The New View Over Atlantis" by John Michell, and "Lines on the Landscape" by Nigel Pennick and Paul Devereux

CONTENTS

INTRODUCTION

On June 30 1921, Herefordshire businessman, Alfred Watkins, was driving along a road in Blackwardine, near Leominster. Attracted by the nearby archeological investigation of a Roman camp, he stopped his car to compare the landscape on either side of the road with the marked features on his map.

Whilst contemplating the landscape around him he saw, in the words of his son, "like a chain of fairy lights", a series of straight alignments of various ancient features, such as standing stones, wayside crosses, hill forts and ancient churches. The discovery, he later wrote, came to him "like a flash".

Enthusiastic commentators since have interpreted it as a mystic vision (*see illustration opposite*), which the methodical and practical Watkins would have certainly indignantly denied. Watkins was not the first person to notice alignments at ancient sites, but he was the first to propose that alignments existed all over the land and, crucially, to give them an appropriate name, *leys*, because of the frequency with which this Saxon place name, meaning a cleared strip of land, occurred along them.

Since he made his discovery public ley lines have become associated with prehistoric trackways, ancient astronomy, UFOs, mysterious earth energy, ghosts, flying shamen and spirits of the dead. What a long, strange trip it's been.

The Royal Forest of Dean, 2000

THE MYSTERY OF LEY LINES
UFOs and strange energies

It's a dull imagination that isn't fired on first hearing of the concept of ley lines. From Alfred Watkins' simple discovery of lost ancient trackways in 1921, ley lines have evolved to encompass a wide field of theory and speculation.

The modern revival in ley hunting was triggered by the post war flying saucer craze. In the 1950s French ufologist Aimé Michell had claimed that sightings of UFOs, when plotted on a map, fell into straight lines which he called 'orthotenies'. One of the earliest alien abductees, Buck Nelson, had written that flying saucer pilots tapped into lines of magnetic force in the earth to power their craft. Then, in the early 1960s, ex-RAF pilot Tony Wedd, an enthusiastic believer in UFOs, put these two fantastic concepts together with Alfred Watkins' leys and thus the ley as a line of magnetic force was born.

The sixties counterculture embraced ley lines as part of the cultural revolution and the mystical energy lines quickly became the accepted explanation for leys. Before long dowsers claimed to be able to locate hidden energies at ancient sacred sites such as stone circles and standing stones and eventually claimed to be able to dowse the leys that run between them.

THE FIRST LEY HUNTERS
the Straight Track Club

Watkins spent the following years verifying his initial discovery. He travelled extensively in his home county of Herefordshire photographing sites and accumulating an impressive collection of data, which was published in 1925 as *The Old Straight Track*.

He had concluded that the alignment of prominent hills and the ranks of minor mark points between them represented the routes of prehistoric traders carrying salt, pottery and flint. Ignored by the archaeologists of the day it quickly became a best seller and ley hunting soon became a popular pastime.

Within two years the *Straight Track Postal Portfolio Club* was established by ley enthusiasts to investigate leys for themselves. They circulated their researches in a series of portfolios, which were posted in turn to each member. Many leys were proposed, some of which clearly could never have been traders' tracks and soon members started to question Watkins' key discoveries.

Though many strange theories were proposed for leys, no-one seemed to be any closer to finding a satisfactory explanation. With the outbreak of war in 1939 the Club eventually broke up and Watkins' theory was largely forgotten until the 1960s.

Opposite: Alfred Watkins announces the first ever excursion of the Straight Track Club in Hereford in 1933. A splendid time is guaranteed for all.

THE STRAIGHT TRACK CLUB

SUMMER
MEETING

HEREFORD

Thursday, July 13th to
Monday, July 17th, 1933

Leader of Excursions :
ALFRED WATKINS, 5, Harley Court, Hereford.

Deputy Leader of Excursions and Local Hon. Secretary :
W. H. McKAIG, "Oban," Ledbury Road, Hereford.

Hon. Secretary of Club :
M. C. CARR-GOMM, 57, Abbey House, Victoria Street,
London, S.W.1

ASTRONOMICAL ALIGNMENTS
Watkins, Lockyer, Thom and Stonehenge

Sir Norman Lockyer's research in 1901 on the astronomical orientation of ancient temples showed that certain alignments of stones through the centre of Stonehenge had been arranged to point to the moment of sunrise or sunset on particular days of the year.

Alfred Watkins lost no time in revisiting Stonehenge to follow up what Lockyer had not fully developed, the evidence of other mark points for those astronomical alignments. He found good evidence for four such alignments. More corroboration was to come from Admiral Boyle Sommerville, a Straight Track Club member who noted that several stone rows, circles and dolmens in the Hebrides and in Ireland were precisely aligned to sunrise and sunset on significant days in the year. Such alignments then continued in straight lines to marks, notches, cairns or earthworks on or near hilltops several miles away.

A similar alignment can be seen at Newgrange, in Ireland where the passage to the central chambers of the tomb is oriented towards the point of midwinter sunrise. On the same line lie two decorated kerbstones, a burial mound and one of the stones of the surrounding stone circle (*see pages 42-43*).

Opposite: The midsummer solstice alignment from the centre of Stonehenge.

THE HOLY LINES OF GERMANY
the work of Teudt and Heinsch

Alignments of ancient sacred sites are not confined to Britain. In 1939 the German Josef Heinsch published a paper, *Principles of Prehistoric Sacred Geography*, in which he spoke of a lost magic principle by which holy sites had been located in the remote past. The sites, he claimed, were points on the lines of great geometrical figures that had been constructed to certain fixed angles and units of measurement based on simple fractions of the earth's dimensions. This ancient pattern, he said, was still recognisable in the present landscape because of the adoption of pagan sites by the Christian Church.

Watkins had a second German contemporary, Wilhelm Teudt, an evangelical parson who claimed that a rock-cut chapel in the Externsteine, one of several natural twisted stacks of rock in West Saxony, was a solar observatory and that 'astronomical lines', linking numerous sacred sites radiated outwards throughout northern Germany.

He called these lines *heilige Linien* or holy lines, but the adoption of Teudt's questionable theories by Himmler during the rise of the Nazis led to his ideas being consigned to obscurity.

Opposite: Ley hunting in Germany. Cardinal alignments of sacred sites by one of Wilheim Teudt's contemporaries.

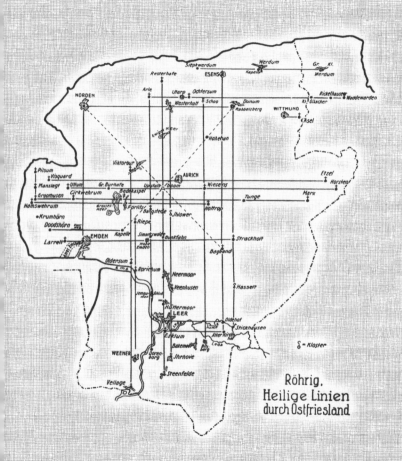

Röhrig,
Heilige Linien
durch Ostfriesland

PATHWAYS TO THE GODS
Nasca lines, Inca ceques and Bolivian tracks

———————————

Real physical evidence for the old straight track is abundant in South America. The most well known straight landscape lines can be seen at Nasca in Peru. Dozens of straight lines are laid out across the desert. Their true purpose remains a mystery.

Elsewhere in the Peruvian desert other straight lines made from small heaps of stones link low mounds with prominent hills. Near Lima straight lines radiate from a central space like the spokes of a wheel. They are not roads, but link together ancient sacred places called *wak'as*.

17th century Jesuit texts record the one-time existence of invisible lines radiating out from the centre of the ancient Inca city of Cuzco. These lines are known as *ceques* and were believed to be sacred pathways. Today they are only visible as alignments of shrines and churches exactly in the manner of English leys.

In Bolivia long straight tracks can be found running for miles across the undulating Andean altiplano from hills and piles of stones to white painted chapels on the summits of low hills. The lines and tracks have a sacred and religious significance.

Opposite: Etch-a-Sketch, Peruvian style. A section of the Nazca pampa, covered in straight lines, trapezoids and zoomorphic images. For an idea of scale, the condor has a wingspan of over 350 feet.

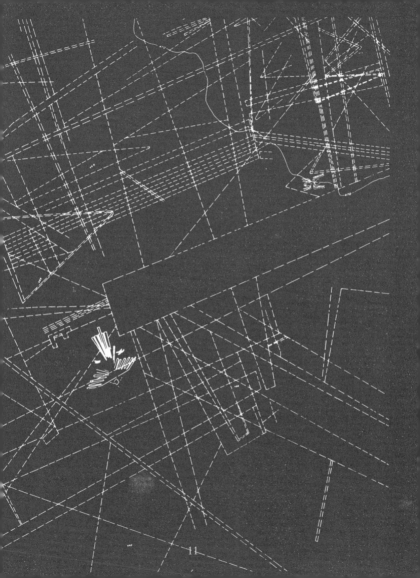

11

ROAD, MOUND AND MERIDIAN
alignments of the ancient Americans

———————

Elsewhere in the Americas fragments of ancient straight road systems can still be traced. Whether all these various straight roads or lines have a common purpose is not clear, but a unifying factor is that they invariably link holy or sacred places.

In Yucatan, in Mexico, the Maya constructed dead straight ceremonial roads through the jungle called *sacbeob*. In New Mexico infrared satellite photography has revealed a system of dead straight roads centred on Chaco Canyon, the site of many ancient ruined ceremonial and religious buildings known as *kivas*.

The road system is a mystery as the Anasazi people who built them had neither the wheel nor the horse. Rather than linking communities the roads connect specific places in the landscape which suggests a symbolic purpose.

Recently an American archaeologist has identified an alignment of ancient Anasazi cities along a north south meridian over several hundred miles long, part of which is marked by the Chacoan Great North Road.

Prehistoric linear earthworks in Wisconsin (*main picture*) have astronomical orientations and in Mississippi ancient Indian circular and effigy mounds were laid out in linear ranges (*side pictures*).

DREAM ROADS
aboriginal songlines

Evidence for invisible sacred pathways can be found in the religious beliefs of aboriginal peoples across the world. In Australia the beliefs and knowledge of the aborigines can be found in the traditional stories of the Dreaming.

This was a mythical period in aborigine history set at the dawn of time when mythological creators or gods emerged from the featureless earth and began to wander aimlessly across it. Every place where they camped, made fires, dug for water or performed ceremonies they marked with a natural feature, such as a rock, hill or watercourse. Those wanderings across country are preserved in the songs and stories of present day aborigine tribes.

Each tribe has possession of one part of the whole creation myth and the finishing place of a 'line of songs' is where the myths and songs change hands to another tribe and thus form a mythical tribal boundary. The invisible lines linking the various songs and stories are the lines of communication between the tribes which when drawn together represent a mythical map of Australia.

Opposite: The lines linking aborigine stories form the outline of the Australian continent (after David Mowaljartai). Below is the Rainbow Snake whose epic journey across country is recorded in aborigine myth.

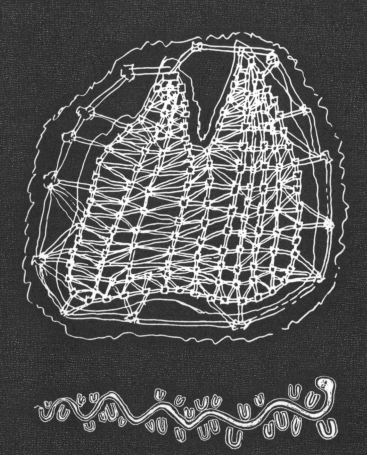

DRAGON LINES & FAIRY PASSES
enhancing good luck from China to Ireland

Invisible straight lines can also be found in other parts of the world. The Chinese science of geomancy, known as *feng shui*, was originally developed for determining the best location for a tomb.

Feng shui tradition believes that harmony in landscape and life can be achieved through the manipulation of natural forces that course through 'veins' in the earth. These forces, in certain circumstances, manifest themselves as *lung mei*, or dragon lines, which run in straight lines. Lung mei are also spirit paths, as the Chinese believed that spirits preferred to travel by the straightest route. Thus it was considered unlucky to build a house at the end of a straight road or path.

In a similar tradition the fairies or 'little people' of Irish folklore had their favoured routes which ran straight between fairy forts, or *raths*, circular earthworks of known antiquity. These fairy roads are known as passes and are sometimes, but not always, marked by physical roads. It was considered unlucky and even dangerous to build on or to block a fairy pass. Calamity would befall anyone who did so.

Opposite: The Forbidden City, centre of old Peking, lies on a dragon line that passes through the city gate, the Emperor's palace and a sacred mound.

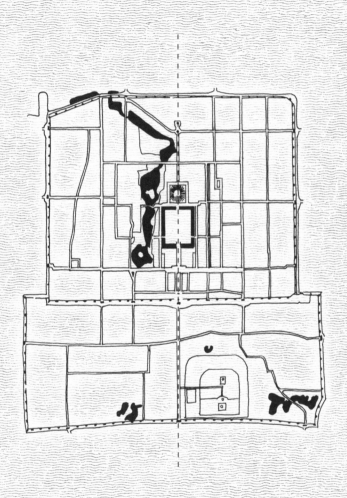

MEDIEVAL ALIGNMENTS
the siting of churches and cathedrals

Many of Alfred Watkins' leys linked medieval churches and churchyards, and while he argued that ancient churches were built on earlier pagan sites this could not always be proven. But there was a tradition of straight alignment in the Middle Ages.

In the Netherlands it was decreed by law that the dead had to be carried for burial along a specially designated road called a *dodweg* or 'death road'. These were invariably dead straight.

In Germany in the 10th and 11th centuries it was the deliberate practice to lay out towns to a sacred geometric scheme. A cathedral was built at the centre of the town and four churches were erected in the cardinal directions, forming a cross. Often the churches were linked to the cathedral by straight roads, and sometimes existing pagan sites were incorporated into these Christian alignments. At Speyer the axis of the cathedral continues as the main street or ceremonial way to the city gate and points towards the prominent Kalmit mountain.

In England the cities of York and Cambridge boast impressive alignments of seven medieval churches (*see pages 44-45*).

Opposite: A church line and pilgrimage route in Zurich, Switzerland. Fraumunster, the bridge, Wasserkirche and the Grossmunster align with a blue stone (centre of picture), the geomantic centre of the city. (J Murer, 1576).

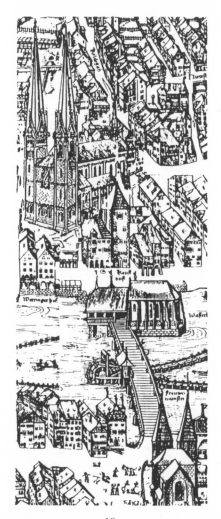

THE JOURNEY OF THE SOUL
funeral paths and corpse ways

———————————

The tradition of carrying a corpse for burial along a special road is prevalent throughout Western Europe and may be linked to the fear of ghosts and wandering spirits.

Dutch death roads may have been straight, but contemporary German death roads are seldom straight and neither are the medieval funeral paths and corpse ways of the British Isles. In the Middle Ages some villages and hamlets were required by Church law to bury their dead at the nearest church that held the burial right. Funeral parties would use a designated route, known as a 'burial path', 'coffin path' or 'church road' to convey the coffin.

There are many traditions and beliefs bound up in the rites of death and burial, and many protective measures were undertaken before, during and after the funeral to protect the living from the spirits of the deceased. It is possible that the straight funeral route was deliberately avoided so as to confuse the spirit of the dead person if it tried to return home, as spirits were believed to prefer travel in straight lines. The belief in straight spirit travel occurs throughout the world.

Opposite: The last journey. Burial Lane at Feckenham, Worcestershire. One of hundreds of abandoned funeral paths across England.

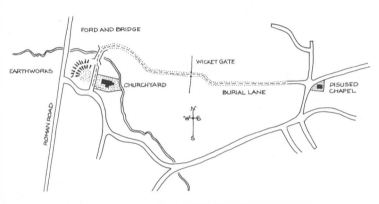

21

SPIRIT PATHS & GHOST ROADS
the universal concept of straight spirit flight

As we have seen, the belief in straight spirit travel is prevalent across the world. German death roads may not have been straight, but *Geisterwege* or 'ghost roads' most certainly are.

German folklore records that ghost roads always run straight over mountains and valleys and through marshes and start and end at cemeteries. Elsewhere in Germany tradition recalls other straight spirit paths such as the *Leichenflugbahn* or 'Flightpath of the Corpses' in East Prussia, where on certain nights the dead from the cemeteries situated at each end of the line travel to visit one other. Houses built on the line regularly suffer damage on the nights when the spirits fly.

Halfway across the world in Columbia the Kogi Indians, descendants of the extinct Tairona culture, tend the ruins of great cities in the jungle reaches of Santa Marta. Straight stone causeways link the cities as do other invisible spirit roads. The Kogi shamans when in trance regularly travel along these invisible routes. Their courses are preserved in the linear markings on a standing stone in one of their villages.

Opposite: Above: The paths of Chuckchee shamen during fly-agaric hallucinations (from Wasson 1971). Below: A Chuckchee map of the journey of a human soul to the spirit world.

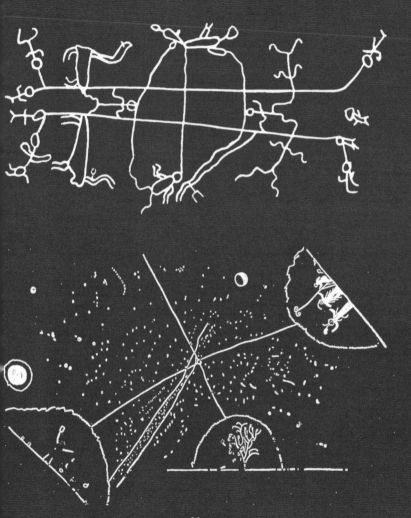

SUPERNATURAL HIGHWAYS
linear hauntings and apparitions

An explanation for some leys might be the spirit path, as ghostly linear journeys are common in folklore. Examples include the wandering ghostly monk who makes regular journeys between a church and a haunted house, phantom coaches that speed along sections of old road at night, or spectral funeral processions taking the same route to a churchyard year after year.

Sometimes these spirit paths have a physical counterpart, by way of an old paved track, or can be successfully plotted on the map to show their straightness.

In many parts of Britain ghostly Black Dogs haunt stretches of old highways. Before the war Theo Brown plotted the sightings of Black Dogs in Devon and Cornwall on the map and found that straight lines could be drawn through many of them.

Theories about ley lines are as numerous as the leys themselves, but if one studies the evidence closely for archaic linear features across the world it is clear that there is a definite link between straightness, death and burial and spirit travel. It is in this direction that modern ley hunting is now heading.

Opposite: Above: A spectral Black Dog that takes the straight path (from a pamphlet, 1577). Below: A classic encounter with a phantom coach. Note the absence of the horses' heads.

WHAT IS A LEY LINE?
an introduction to examples which follow

The following pages describe and list alignments of the types discussed in this book.

Included are some of Alfred Watkins' own discovered leys, some of a similar nature that have been found by modern ley hunters inspired by Watkins' vision, astronomical alignments, acknowledged prehistoric alignments of sites and stones, sacred pathways, funeral routes, death roads and spirit paths.

All of the alignments given here have at one time or another come under the heading of 'ley lines'. From these lists it is clear that there is no one single type of landscape line that can definitively be called a ley, but these examples demonstrate mankind's continual obsession with the straight line or path in the landscape.

I have selected examples that take in some of the more famous prehistoric sites in Britain and others for those who enjoy combining their interest in megalithic sites with walking in the country. In addition I have included examples from Ireland, France, Belgium and Holland, which I hope will show that ley hunting is not confined to Britain.

Opposite: What is a ley line? Strange energies between sacred sites, lines to the Sun and the Moon, or the paths of disembodied spirits? (Ulrich Magin).

A HOLY HILL ALIGNMENT
Wilmington Ley, Sussex, England

Alfred Watkins deduced from place name evidence that his proposed Stone Age ley surveyors were probably called 'dod' men. Looking for illustrations of potential ancient surveyors he seized upon the antique chalk hill figure of the Long Man of Wilmington as a representation of the ley man. It is fitting therefore that the Long Man should lie on a ley.

The first ley marker is the 12th century St. Mary's and St. Peter's church in the village of Wilmington, Sussex. Legend says it is connected by a tunnel to the crypt of the next ley point, the Norman Wilmington Priory. Legends of tunnels often occur on leys. The third marker is the Long Man, a 237ft long, featureless outline of a human figure holding a long staff in each hand (Watkins' surveyor's staffs); the date of the figure is uncertain, but is possibly pre-Roman. The top of the hill on which the Long Man lies is marked by the fourth point, Windover Hill round barrow, 135ft in diameter. The line can be extended further north where it crosses a hard-to-find Bronze Age bowl barrow. Many leys start or end at a prominent hill.

Opposite: Watkins adopted the Long Man of Wilmington as his ley surveyor, or Dodman. To the left we see the descendents of Dod (after Watkins), and to the right are some of the many recorded versions of the Long Man.

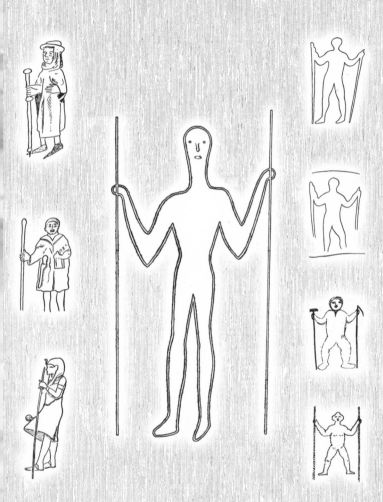

CHURCH LEYS IN OXFORD
the axes of the town defined

In *The Old Straight Track* Alfred Watkins draws attention to the alignments of churches in some of Britain's old cities, notably Hereford, Bristol, Oxford and London.

In Oxford two church leys cross at St Martin's Carfax at the centre of the city and in fact define the two main axes of Oxford, Queen Street - Carfax - High Street and Magdalen Street - Cornmarket Street - St. Aldate Street, running approximately north-south and east-west.

The north-south line includes St. Giles (*a*), St. Mary Magdalen (*b*), St. Michael's (*c*), St. Martin's Carfax (*d*), St. Aldate (*e*) and crosses the Thames at 'Oskna Ford', now Folly Bridge (*4*).

The east-west line links St. Peter's in the Castle (*h*) (now demolished), St. Martin's Carfax (*d*), All Saints (*g*) and St. Mary the Virgin (*f*). St Martin's Carfax lies on the highest part of the old city and was once the assembly point for council, justice and commerce.

The streets that follow these two lines deviate to avoid the churches in a manner noticed by Watkins in many other leys.

Opposite: Did these leys define the street pattern of Oxford? Alfred Watkins' own map of the medieval church alignments in the city of Oxford.

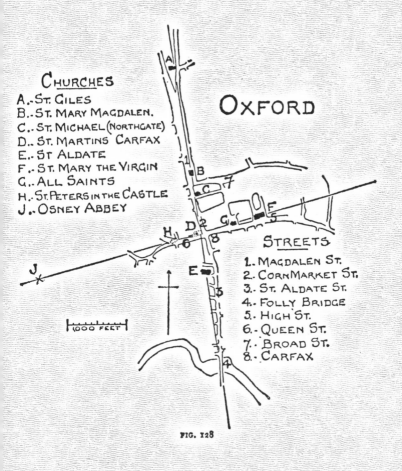

CHURCHES
A.. ST. GILES
B.. ST. MARY MAGDALEN.
C.. ST. MICHAEL (NORTHGATE)
D.. ST. MARTINS CARFAX
E.. ST ALDATE
F.. ST. MARY THE VIRGIN
G.. ALL SAINTS
H.. ST. PETERS IN THE CASTLE
J.. OSNEY ABBEY

OXFORD

STREETS
1.. MAGDALEN ST.
2.. CORNMARKET ST.
3.. ST. ALDATE ST.
4.. FOLLY BRIDGE
5.. HIGH ST.
6.. QUEEN ST.
7.. BROAD ST.
8.. CARFAX

1000 FEET

FIG. 128

A SCOTTISH ROYAL LEY
a line of kings, Argyllshire, Scotland

The Kilmartin valley, in Argyllshire, Scotland, is home to an extra-ordinary concentration of prehistoric monuments dating from 4000 to 1200 BC.

The dominant feature of Kilmartin is a straight line of burial cairns that follows the contour of the valley. The sites include an unnamed cairn north of Crinian Moss, the small and denuded Rowanfield cist (whose axis points along the ley), Ri Cruin or the King's Circle, a well-preserved prehistoric tomb dating from 4000 BC containing three chambers and carved stones, a standing stone incised with cup and ring marks, Nether Largie South chambered cairn, 130ft in diameter and dating from 3500 BC and the tomb of a king or queen, the site of a chambered cairn destroyed at the turn of the century, and two more royal tombs, Nether Largie mid-Cairn, 100ft across, and Nether Largie North, dating from 3000BC.

The final tomb on the line is Glebe Cairn, once the tallest on the line. If projected further north the ley passes through the hill fort of Dun na Nighinn and terminates at the hill fort and natural pyramidal peak of Dun Chonnalaich.

Opposite: The royal burial mounds of the Kilmartin valley trace a straight line of eleven sites that lead to a sacred mountain peak.

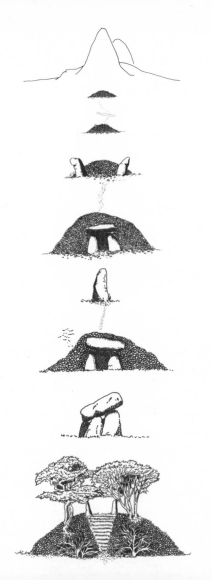

A SUNRISE LINE
Stonehenge, Wiltshire, England

Perhaps the most famous of all ancient astronomical alignments is the summer solstice alignment at Stonehenge, Wiltshire.

On the longest day of the year, when viewed from the centre of the monument, the sun can be seen rising over the outlying Heel Stone between the massive uprights that form the central ring. The earth banked Avenue that leads away from Stonehenge is aligned in the same direction for several hundred yards.

The antiquary William Stukeley first noted this strange phenomenon in 1740 when he wrote that the axis of Stonehenge and the Avenue is directed to the north-east 'whereabouts the sun rises when the days are longest'.

Alfred Watkins noted in *The Old Straight Track* that the alignment also passes through two Bronze Age barrows to the southwest of Stonehenge.

Stukeley noted another barrow once visible on the skyline on Haradon Hill and lining up with the Avenue marking the point on the horizon where the summer solstice sun would rise.

Opposite: Above: Alignments around Stonehenge (after Alfred Watkins). Below: The Avenue pointing away from Stonehenge to a barrow on the distant Haradon Hill that marks the summer solstice sunrise.

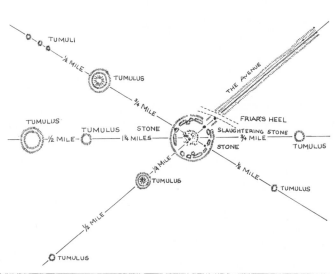

TUMULI

TUMULUS

¼ MILE

¾ MILE

THE AVENUE

FRIAR'S HEEL

TUMULUS

TUMULUS

STONE

SLAUGHTERING STONE

½ MILE

¼ MILES

¾ MILE

TUMULUS

STONE

¼ MILE

TUMULUS

½ MILE

TUMULUS

½ MILE

TUMULUS

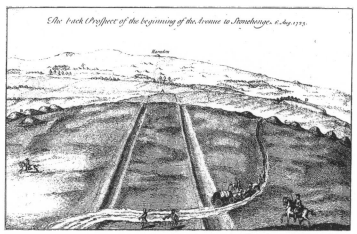

The back Prospect of the beginning of the Avenue to Stonehenge. 6. Aug. 1723.

Haraden

35

ORCADIAN LEYS
Orkney, Scotland

Orkney is famous for its fine collection of megalithic monuments: the Ring of Brodgar henge and circle of stones, the Stones of Stennes, the remains of another henge and stone circle, and the vast chambered mound of Maes Howe.

The latter has its passage oriented directly to the point on the horizon where the midwinter sun sets. To reinforce this alignment a standing stone was erected over 900 yards away at Barnhouse as a foresight. Magnus Spence, an Orcadian school-master, first noted this and other solar alignments in 1894.

A line linking the Watchstone, an 18ft high monolith and Maes Howe points to the equinox sunrise. These alignments can be clearly seen both on the map and on the ground.

Alignments upon the Ring of Brodgar point to hills where fires were once lit to mark the Celtic festivals of Beltane (1st May) and Samhain (1st Nov). Alexander Thom, who surveyed the sites in the 1970's, found alignments to the moon from the Ring of Brodgar.

Opposite: Astronomical and topographical alignments underlie the sacred geometry of Orkney. Above: The principle alignments around Maes Howe (after Spence). Below: The passage of Maes Howe aligns to midwinter sunset.

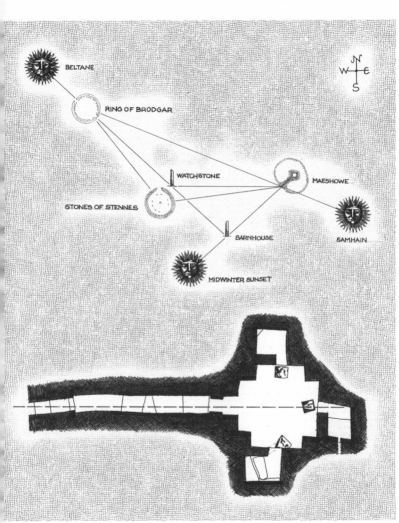

BELTANE

RING OF BRODGAR

WATCHSTONE

MAESHOWE

STONES OF STENNES

SAMHAIN

BARNHOUSE

MIDWINTER SUNSET

N
W E
S

37

THE KENNET AVENUE
Avebury, Wiltshire, England

When the antiquary William Stukeley wrote about the Avebury megaliths in the 18th century he interpreted the complex of huge standing stones as a gigantic serpent temple; the now lost Beckhampton avenue being the tail, the henge and the stone circles its coiled body, and the Kennet Avenue and the Sanctuary on Overton Hill, the neck and head.

Since these fanciful interpretations, writers and archaeologists have referred to the remaining Kennet Avenue as 'sinuous'. It is not. Close inspection reveals that the two parallel lines of megaliths were built in discrete and straight sections over a long period of time. Furthermore, votive offerings and human burials were placed at the points where the avenue changes direction and alongside the outer edges, thus confirming a connection between the lines and death rituals.

The avenue today is largely a restoration and consists of two lines of evocatively shaped megaliths that define a sacred pathway between the Sanctuary and the Avebury henge. Archaeological investigations have revealed that people walked along the outsides of the avenue and not between the rows of stones. Was that route perhaps preserved for the spirits of the dead?

Opposite: Two of William Stukeley's engravings of Avebury from 1743.

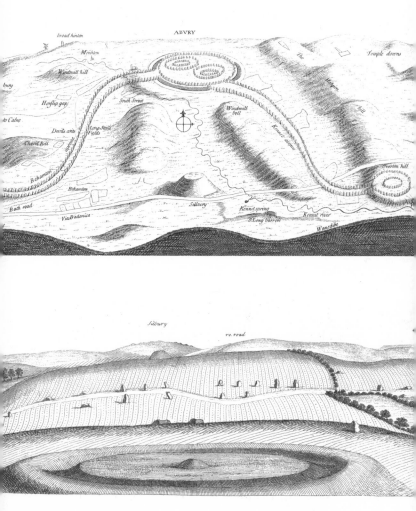

ABVRY

broad hinton

Monkton

Windmill hill

bury

Horslip gap

to Calne

Devils coits

Long Stones fields

Cherill hill

Bekamton

Bekamton

Bath road

Via Badonica

South Street

Windmill holl

Kennet source

Silbury

Kennet spring

S. Long barrow

Kennet river

The

Temple downs

Hill

Overton hill

Wandike

Silbury

vo. road

39

PATHWAY TO THE SUN
Warwickshire and Worcestershire, England

A Warwickshire legend tells of a burial path that once existed over Brailes Hill. The path was said to run for 23 miles to Bredon Hill in neighbouring Worcestershire - a long way for a funeral!

An alignment of sites runs from Brailes to Bredon Hill that might be the origin of the burial path legend. It runs due west from Castle Hill in Brailes, a reshaped natural hill that may have been a Norman castle, over Dover's Hill, the possible site of a turf maze, through Saintbury cross, a crossroads at Hinton Cross, an earthwork at Elmley Castle, and onto the Banbury Stone, an elephantine shaped mass of rock at the edge of an Iron Age hill fort on Bredon Hill.

Projected westwards the line bisects the grand Iron Age British Camp on the Malvern ridge and marks the equinoctial sunset.

The burial path referred to in the legend may be the ancient pilgrim's trackway, now marked by roads and public footpaths, that snakes around the course of the alignment passing burial places along its route and skirting the lower slopes of Brailes Hill on its way to Bredon.

Opposite: The equinoctial sun sets behind British Camp on the Malverns, in line with the Banbury Stone and lookout tower on Bredon Hill (Adam Dutton).

BOYNE VALLEY LEYS
County Meath, Ireland

Three enormous Neolithic chambered mounds, Newgrange, Knowth and Dowth, dominate the Boyne valley in Co Meath, Ireland. Newgrange contains a passage and central chamber which is illuminated by the midwinter rising sun, Knowth has two passages aligned directly east and west and Dowth has two passages, one of which is aligned directly on Newgrange. The Dowth alignment is augmented by two of the standing stones in the circle surrounding the Newgrange mound, which lie exactly on the alignment. In a similar fashion, two more of the stones in the circle fall on a line drawn through an outlying burial mound, Newgrange and Knowth.

Both leys cross at a stone in the central chamber of Newgrange that archaeologists have designated R21, and from this stone lines run to each of the surrounding stones in the circle pointing to astronomical and topographical features. R21 also aligns with the engraved kerb stone at the entrance to Newgrange and a kerb stone at the rear. Both are marked with straight vertical grooves which align with the passage and the midwinter sunrise.

Opposite: Alignments through Newgrange. 1. Winter solstice sunrise. 2. Winter solstice sunset. 3. Summer solstice sunrise. 7. North-south meridian. 8. To Knowth. 9. To Dowth.

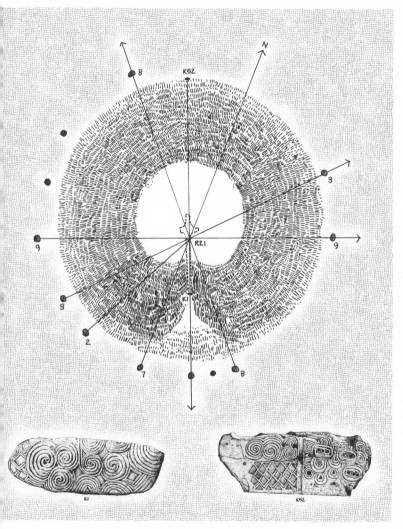

K52

N

8

3

9   RZ1   9

3

2

7   K1   8

K1   K52

YORK MINSTER LEY
York, England

Situated within the city walls of York is a medieval church ley. This alignment is spectacularly visible from the tower of York Minster.

The best way to walk the ley is from its starting point, a spit of land between the Foss and Ouse rivers, which was once Templar land. The ley passes through the site of St. George's chapel, a Templar building, the Norman castle, Clifford's Tower, with its 11th century chapel, the spired church of St. Mary's, dating from the 11th century (now York Heritage Centre), and on to the 15th century All Saints Pavement, a church built on the site of earlier 11th and 7th century churches. All Saints is the oldest church on the line and sits at the crossroads at the centre of the city.

The next sites along the line are the 14th century St. Samson's church, now a Senior Citizen's Centre and the Minster itself, St. Peter's cathedral. The ley passes directly below the 11th century tower at the crossing of the nave and transepts.

The line terminates at the 13th century Archbishop's Palace chapel, but is inaccessible to the public.

Opposite: York Minster rises above the roofs of medieval York. The principle site on an alignment of seven ecclesiastical buildings.

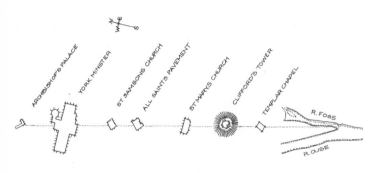

ARCHBISHOP'S PALACE · YORK MINSTER · ST SAMSONS CHURCH · ALL SAINTS PAVEMENT · ST MARYS CHURCH · CLIFFORD'S TOWER · TEMPLAR CHAPEL · R. FOSS · R. OUSE

THE FAIRY STEPS
Cumbria, England

Supernatural encounters are reported on the corpse road from Arndale to Beetham church in Cumbria. The path, which consists of a series of straight sections, follows a dead straight course from Hazelslack Tower Farm, named after the ruined stone fortress that still stands on the farm, to the Fairy Steps.

At Whin Scar the straight corpse road is forced to make a series of dog-leg turns as it ascends the scar in two flights of stone steps. The second flight is known locally as the Fairy Steps and is an impossibly steep rock-cut stairway at the bottom of a very narrow gully. The idea that pall-bearers could manoeuvre a coffin up this cleft is hard to credit.

It is at the Fairy Steps where tradition has it that your wish will be granted by the fairies if you can skip up the stairway without touching the sides. The author has attempted this feat without success. In places the cleft is as narrow as a foot at shoulder height.

Those with the second sight are believed to be able to witness the fairy folk skipping up the steps.

Opposite: The impossibly narrow Fairy Steps in Cumbria. Skipping fairies not shown.

THE MENHIRS OF CARNAC
Brittany, France

The best known of the Breton megalithic sites are the multiple lines of huge standing stones all near the village of Carnac in southern Brittany. The largest group of stone rows is at Kermario.

The cromlechs that stood at both ends of the long rows are now gone but a restored passage mound still stands in line with the southernmost stone row. Cromlechs are spacious rings of close-set standing stones that were probably used for open air rituals connected with death and burial.

The next largest group, at Le Menec, has twelve roughly parallel stone rows running between two egg-shaped cromlechs. Many of the original stones are missing, robbed for road building and the like. The stone rows may have marked ritual processional ways or death roads between the funerary sites.

The Kerlescan rows, north of Carnac, also run to a cromlech. At the western end, alongside the cromlech there is a *tertre tumulaire*, a rectangular burial mound. Kermario means 'place of the dead' and Kerlescan means 'place of burning', an indication of activities that once may have taken place at the ends.

Opposite: Ranks of huge megalithic mark the sacred paths between two egg-shaped stone rings (plan after Thom).

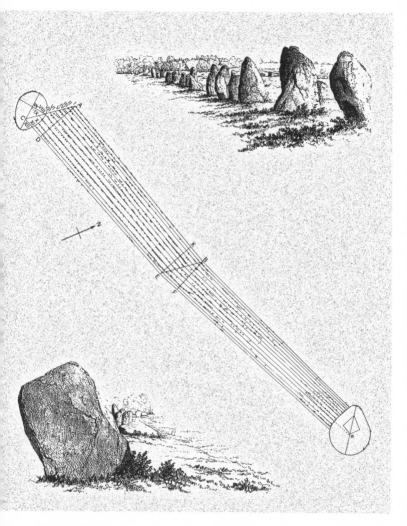

THE STONEHENGE CURSUS LEY
a prehistoric funeral route

The Stonehenge Cursus is a two-mile long rectangular earthen ditched enclosure that lies about half a mile north of Stonehenge itself. The antiquary William Stukeley first noticed it in 1723 when he interpreted it as a Roman racecourse, hence 'cursus'.

The Stonehenge Cursus links a group of round barrows at its western end to a long barrow at its eastern extremity. Alfred Watkins first noted that a line drawn along the straight northern ditch passes through the Cuckoo Stone to the east, a standing stone not marked on the 1:50 000 map.

Excavations by Mrs Cunnington, in the 1930s, revealed the circular henge monument now called Woodhenge, through which to his delight Watkins was able to extend his ley. This alignment was later given archaeological credence in 1947.

The links between straightness and the dead at the Stonehenge Cursus are very persuasive and indeed the Woodhenge excavations revealed the body of a child who had apparently been sacrificed and buried at the centre of the henge. The line can be extended further east to where it strikes the horizon at Beacon Hill, thus finding its Watkinsian terminal point.

Opposite: The enigmatic and almost obliterated Stonehenge cursus points to both the Cuckoo Stone and the centre of Woodhenge.

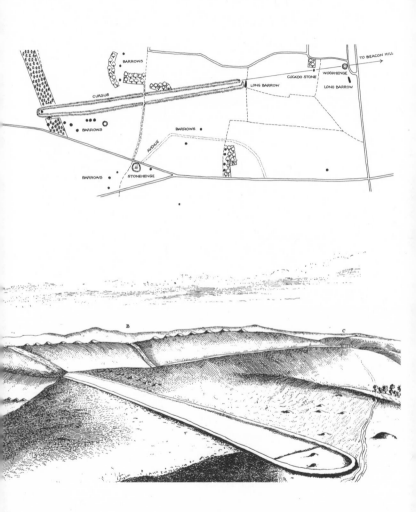

A BELGIAN ALIGNMENT
Wéris, Belgium

This is an alignment of contemporary megalithic monuments that is acknowledged by Belgian archaeologists as deliberate and planned.

Two miles outside the town of Erezée at Bohaimont at Oppagne stands a group of three menhirs, which were re-erected in 1906. The tallest stone is 8ft tall. The line is at right angles to the alignment, which leads northwards to a half-buried allée-couverte (or passage grave) near Wénin. The next site on the line is a 12ft tall menhir built into a wall at the side of the road. This stone had been toppled and buried but was restored in 1947.

Over half a mile further on the line passes over the Dolmen de Wéris, a major dolmen over 36ft long with a huge capstone.

Both dolmens are orientated upon the alignment. Further along the line to the north are the remains of fallen menhirs, broken up at the end of the 19th century. These may have formed another line like the Oppagne group marking the end of the alignment.

Opposite: Megaliths on the Wéris alignment. Above: The ruined dolmen at Wéris. Below: Three menhirs at Oppagne. Etchings by John Palmer.

3. MENHIRS, OPPAGNE

THREE DUTCH DEATH ROADS
Hilversum, Netherlands

Straight medieval doodwegen, or death roads, are still visible in parts of the Netherlands. They were built for the specific purpose of carrying the dead to burial, and their specification and upkeep were the subject of decrees and periodic inspections. Medieval laws forbade the transportation of corpses on other types of road.

This splendid example comes from Westerheide heath between Laren and Hilversum, in north Holland, an area dotted with Bronze Age barrows. Three dead straight doodwegen converge on the isolated St. Janskerhof (St. John's cemetery). The three roads are equally spaced forming a triangle pointing at the chapel of St. John. The present day chapel is only a century old, but it replaced an earlier building said to date from the 1600's or earlier.

The death road from the village of ës-Graveland is believed to have been laid out in 1643. The other two, from the villages of Bussum and Ankerveen, are of uncertain date but are believed to be older. They are not Roman roads as they lie outside the boundaries of the Roman occupation of the Low Countries.

Which brings us to the end of this little book of Leys!

Opposite: Three dead straight doodwgen on the barrow studded Westerheide heath aim in on the isolated churchyard of St. John's chapel.

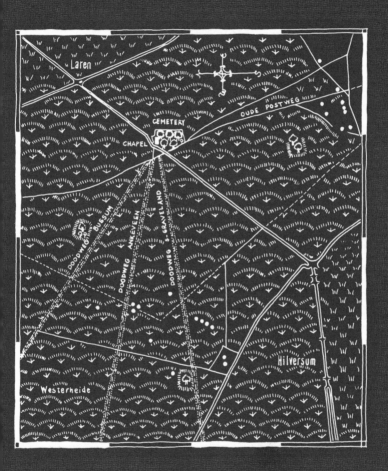

Laren

CEMETERY

CHAPEL

OUDE POSTWEG

BUSSUM

DOODWEG

DOODWEG ANKEVEEN

DOODWEG S. GRAVELAND

Hilversum

Westerheide

APPENDIX OF NOTABLE LEYS

'OSLS' refers to the 1:50 000 Ordinance Survey Landranger Sheet No.

A Cornish Spirit Path (OSLS 203). *St Mary's church, Penzance, Cornwall - Chapel Street, Penzance - Madron church and holy well - section of straight track - cross - Lanyon Quiot dolmen - straight section of road to Trevowhan.*

A Supernatural Highway in the Mendips (OSLS 172). *Cross Keys Inn, Bedminster Down (site of gibbet and appearance of spectral horse) - the haunted driveway to Bishopworth manor house - a haunted stretch of road over Dundry Hill - the ancient spring of Wriggleswell - Pagan Hill (site of Roman temple and votive well) - Pilgrim's Way burial path at Chew Stoke - St Andrew's church - site of a stone circle and holy well - Moreton Cross and St Mary's well - White Cross (suicide burial site) - Harptree parish boundary.*

Two Glastonbury Leys (OSLS 182, 172). Ley 1: *St Benedict's church, Glastonbury - Glastonbury Abbey (axis of abbey is on the ley) - the line of Dod Lane - St Michael's church on Gare Hill - Stonehenge.* Ley 2: *St Nicholas' church, Brockley (tunnel legend) - Holy Trinity church, Burrington - Gorsey Bigsbury henge - Westbury Beacon camp, Mendips - crossroads and mark stone at Yarley - St. Michael's church tower, Glastonbury Tor - St Leonard's church, Butleigh (centre of the Glastonbury Zodiac)*

The First Ley discovered by Alfred Watkins in Herefordshire (OSLR 149). *Croft Ambrey Iron Age hill fort - the line of Croft Lane (1.5 miles long) - mark stone at crossroads at Blackwardine - Risbury Camp - high point at Stretton Grandison (site of a Roman station).*

Burial Lane at Feckenham, Worcestershire. (OSLR 150). *Ham Green hamlet - derelict chapel at Cruise Hill - Burial Lane (street name) - bridleway - iron gate across path - ford and footbridge - road - Feckenham church*

Cerne Abbas Ley, Dorset (OSLR 194). *St Lawrence's church, Holwell in Dorset - tumulus - prehistoric settlement site - The Trendle earthwork enclosure on Giant's Hill - Cerne Abbas abbey ruins - holy well (site of a vision by St Augustine) - St Mary's church, Cerne Abbas.*

Church Path at Gotherington, Gloucs. (OSLR 163). *Shutter Lane, Gotherington - 'Church Walk' footpath - green lane and path through fields - St Michael's, Bishop's Cleeve.*

Coldrum Ley, Kent (OSLR 188). *St. Peter and Paul's, Trosley (large stones set into foundations, axis of church on ley) - Coldrum long barrow (tunnel legend links Trosley church and*

Coldrum barrow) - old track crossing - All Saint's, Snodland (Pilgrim's Way skirts the churchyard) - lost paved ford across the River Medway - St Mary's, Burnham Court - Blue Bell Hill.

The Devil's Arrows, Yorkshire (OSLR 99). Ley 1: *Thornborough henges - Nunwick henge - central Devil's Arrow, Boroughbridge.* Ley 2: *Central and southernmost Devil's Arrows standing stones, Boroughbridge - Cana henge - tumulus at Low Barn - Hutton Moor henge.*

Knowlton Henge Ley, Dorset (OSLR 195). *Bronze Age tumulus - Bronze Age tumulus - Bronze Age tumulus - Knowlton henge (ruined medieval church) - summer solstice sunrise.*

Loanhead of Daviot, Aberdeenshire (OSLR 38). *Loanhead of Daviot recumbent stone circle - stone circle in Daviot churchyard (removed) - New Craig recumbent stone circle.*

London Leys (OSLR 176). Ley 1: *St. Martins-in-the-Fields - St. Mary-le-Strand - St. Clement Danes (pre-conquest and once held by the Knight's Templar) - St. Dunstan's, Fleet Street - site of an ancient mound approximately at Arnold's Circus in Shoreditch (parts of Pall Mall and The Strand fall on the alignment).* Ley 2: *St. Paul's, Covent Garden - The Temple church (a Knight's Templar round church) - St Bride's, Fleet Street - church on Ludgate Hill - church near the Guildhall - St. Stephen's, Coleman Street - St. Botolph's, Bishopsgate (the Temple church and St Bride's are oriented on the ley).* Ley 3: *Temple church - St. Paul's Cathedral (built on Ludgate Hill) - St Helen's Bishopsgate - St. Dunstan's, Stepney - St. Clement Dane's (St Paul's, St Helen's and St Dunstan's all orient closely on the same angle as the ley).*

May Hill Ley, Gloucestershire (OSLR 163). *Giant's Stone long barrow - Wittantree (Saxon moot place) - Bull's Cross (site of appearance of phantom coach and horses) - Painswick church (site of annual 'clipping' ceremony) - May Hill.*

Old Sarum Ley, Wiltshire (OSLR 184). *Stonehenge - Old Sarum (Iron Age earthwork and later medieval cathedral site) - Salisbury Cathedral - Clearbury Ring (Iron Age hill fort) - Frankenbury Camp (Iron Age hill fort) - tumulus on Durrington Down.*

Saintbury Ley and Funeral Path, Gloucestershire (OSLR 150). *Cross and crossroads - straight section of road (once a funeral path) - St. Nicholas church, Saintbury - Bronze Age round barrow - Neolithic long barrow - a pagan Saxon cemetery - Seven Wells farm (a place locally associated with medieval witchcraft).*

Silbury Hill Ley, Wiltshire (OSLR 173). *Bincknoll Castle - a Norman motte and bailey - an ancient well, Broad Hinton - churchyard of St Peter's, Broad Hinton (via the lych gate) - Avebury Henge - Silbury Hill - site of a lost stone circle (noted by Stukeley) - Tan Hill (site of a former fair) - the crossing of an earthwork ditch and the Wansdyke (a post-Roman boundary bank and ditch, phantom funerals have been seen at this point) - Marden henge.*

Stanton Drew, Somerset (OSLR 172). *Alignment 1: Centre of the south-western circle - centre of the Great Circle - Hautville's Quoit - midsummer sunrise point (2000 BC). Alignment 2: Centre of the north-eastern circle - centre of the Great Circle - The Cove (Neolithic portal dolmen) - midwinter sunset point on the horizon (2000BC).*

Sutton Walls Ley, Herefordshire (OSLR 149). *Wellington church - Marden church - Sutton Walls Iron Age hill fort (through sighting notch in ramparts) - churchyard cross at Sutton St. Nicholas church - Western Beggard church.*

Funeral Path at Wick, Worcestershire (OSLR 150). *The old road west out of the village (as existing public footpaths) - crossing over River Avon - field path (pointing directly at Pershore Abbey) - a stile and hollow way - the line of Church Street (formerly Lyce (or corpse) Street) - Pershore Abbey.*

Uffington Ley, Oxfordshire/Berkshire (OSLR 174). *St. Mary's, Uffington - Dragon Hill (a natural conical hill and site of dragon killing legend) - Bronze Age barrow - Uffington Castle Iron Age hill fort (above the White Horse) - tumulus at Parkfarm Down - linear earthwork at Near Down - linear earthwork at Farncombe Down - tumulus east of Preston.*

Winchester Ley, Hampshire (OSLR 185). *Tidbury Ring Iron Age hill fort - remains of a Neolithic long barrow, South Wonston - St. Batholemew's church, Winchester - Hyde Gate (at the site of Hyde Abbey, burial place of Alfred the Great) - Winchester Cathedral - St. Catherine's Hill (Iron Age hill fort and site of turf labyrinth called the Mizmaze).*

Yazor Ley, Herefordshire, Monmouthshire (OSLR 149). *A mark stone on the highway at Yazor church, Herefordshire - the ruined tower of Yazor Old Church - a mark stone in a clump of trees at Mansel Gamage - Monnington Court - a mark stone on the highway at Wilmarston - a hill fort near Whitehouse Farm - a churchyard cross at Capel-y-Ffin, Monmouthshire - a bridle pass over Taren-yr-Esgob - mountain peak of Pen-y-Gader, Black Mountains.*

Hereford Church Ley (OSLR 149). *Aligned section of Portland Street - All Saint's church - Site of St. Owen's church - St. Owen Street - St. Giles' chapel - Eign Road - The Crozen (house on a mound) - site of Saxon burial ground).*

Ley Line Cross, Forest of Dean, Gloucestershire (OS *Outdoor Leisure Map* 14). *Ley 1: Sedbury Stone on Offa's Tump - Coomsbury Wood (high point) - Coldharbour Piece, St. Briavels (circular field with radial field boundaries) - clump of Scots Pines at Cauldwell Farm, Stowe - Staunton Longstone - Longstone, Symond's Yat (natural feature) - Queen Stone, Huntsham (peninsula in the River Wye). Ley 2: Butt Acre, Monmouth (town centre, possible stone or temple site) - Kymin, near Monmouth (high point, earthworks) - Buckstone, Staunton (logan or rocking stone) - Staunton Longstone - Berry Hill crossroads - Cannop crossroads - Hungry Croft, Ruddle - Barrow Hill, Arlingham (on the peninsula in the River Severn horseshoe bend).*